I'm Having a Bad Day

Amaan Ishaq

To Faizaan, my fiery little monkey.

A special thanks to ***James*** *for being the first kid to make a cameo in one of my books! If you'd like your child to make a cameo in an upcoming book, don't forget to visit:*

amaanishaq.com/cameo-kids

FIRST EDITION

Pam was excited. Mom had asked what she and her little brother Jam wanted for dinner, and she knew exactly what to get. "Tacos!"

"What?! No! Not tacos! I don't want tacos!" Jam cried out. "Why can't we just get pizza?!"

Pam was annoyed because Jam got to choose the last time.

"Sorry Jam, but it's *my* choice and we are ***not*** getting pizza. We're having tacos."

"FINE! Eat your tacos! Do whatever you want! I don't care! I don't want anything!" Jam screamed, before storming off.

'What does he have against tacos?' Pam wondered.

But it wasn't about the tacos.

EARLIER THAT MORNING...

'What a lovely day,' Jam thought as he woke up that morning. Jam loved the feeling of waking up on a Saturday. No alarms, no rush, just opening your eyes whenever they feel like opening.

And that's about the time his day stopped being so lovely.

"Jam? Why aren't you ready for school yet?" Pam called out.

"School? We don't go to school on Saturdays, silly. That would be illegal. We could go to jail if we did that." said Jam.

"Jam, it's *Tuesday*."

Jam's eyes nearly popped right out as he realized she was right.

“Hurry up, we have to leave in five minutes,” said Pam.

In the next five minutes, Jam somehow managed to brush his teeth, change his clothes, gulp down his breakfast, grab his bag and hurry out the door.

Unfortunately, he was in such a rush that when he changed his clothes, he forgot to change out of his pajama pants.

By the time he realized, he was already at school.

When Jam got to class, he was so worried about everyone noticing his pajama pants that he didn't even notice when the teacher called on him.

"Jam, what do you think the answer is?" she said.

Answer? He didn't even know what the *question* was. 'There's a map on the board. Maybe we're talking about countries,' Jam thought. He decided to try his luck and guess.

"Canada," he answered.

The teacher stared blankly at Jam before finally responding, "No, Jam, I’m sorry, but monkeys do not like to eat... *Canada*."

The whole class burst out laughing.

And then they noticed Jam’s pajama pants and laughed even harder. Jam was so embarrassed.

Art class was even worse.

Jam had painted a picture of a bee. But just as he put the finishing touches on his artwork, he noticed there were now *two* bees.

Jam was puzzled, because he was sure he had only painted one.

And then the second bee flew off of Jam’s painting and landed right on top of his head.

Jam managed to swat the bee away, but not before knocking over the paint and splattering it everywhere.

The teacher was ***not*** pleased when she saw the mess he made.

Jam didn't have any spare clothes to change into, so the teacher made him wear the classroom's emergency shirt instead.

Unfortunately for Jam, the classroom's emergency shirt was a *sack*.

By the time Jam got home, he was feeling totally defeated. He plopped himself down on the couch next to Pam.

He was about to tell her all about his terrible day when Mom called out,

"What do you kids want to eat for dinner tonight?"

Jam's eyes lit up. After such a long, hard day, Jam knew just the thing to turn it around. Pizza! Delicious, cheesy, yummy pizza. Finally, something good would come from this terrible day.

But before he could open his mouth, Pam blurted out...

"Tacos!"

Pam marched over to Jam's room to confront her little brother.

But when she got there, he wasn't fuming mad anymore. Instead, he was lying in his bed, crying.

"Are... you okay?" asked Pam.

"No!" Jam yelled back.

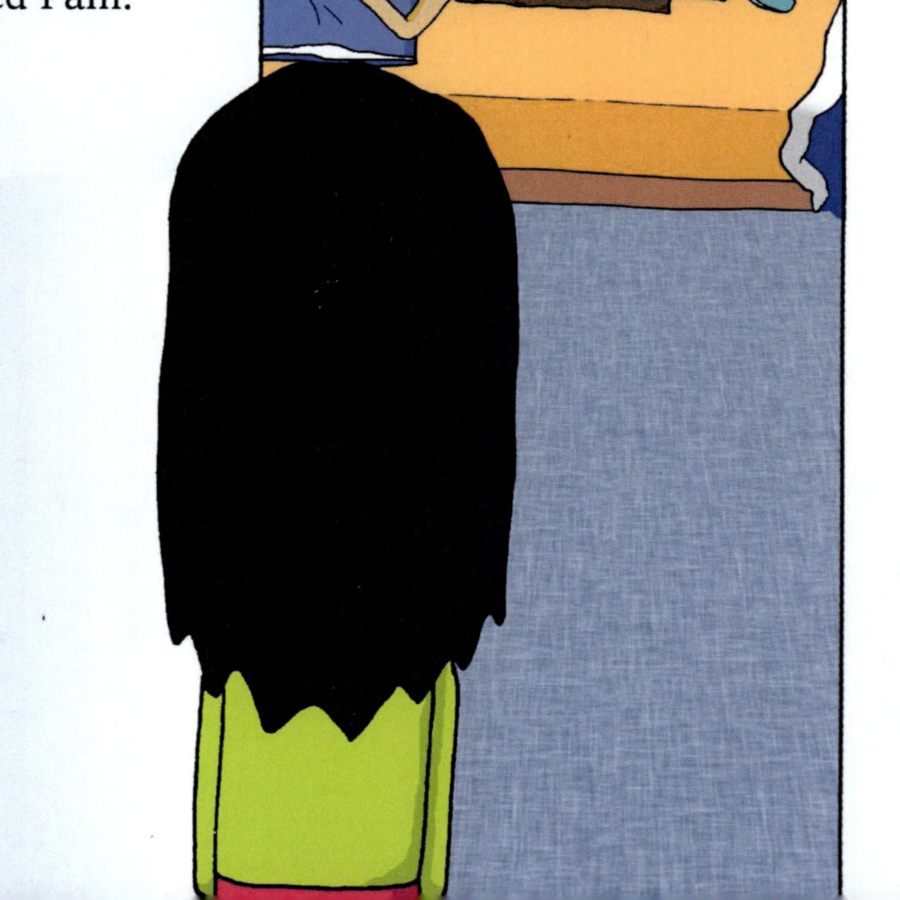

“What’s wrong? I thought you liked tacos?” said Pam.

“I don’t care about tacos! Just do whatever you want!” said Jam.

Pam could see that Jam was really upset. Luckily, she knew just the thing to help him feel better.

"How about for dessert, we have ice cream? I'll even give you one of my scoops," Pam suggested.

"No! I don't want anything! Just leave me alone!" Jam snapped back.

Pam couldn't believe it. If the magical power of ice cream couldn't help Jam feel better, what could? She had no idea how to help him.

And that's when she realized, she didn't even know what was wrong.

“Jam, what exactly happened today?” Pam asked.

Jam was still upset, but he was tired of yelling. He didn't want to fight anymore, so he decided to talk.

"It all started this morning..." said Jam.

And then he told Pam all about his terrible day.

"Wow, I had no idea you were having such a bad day," said Pam. "I'm really sorry, Jam. I'm sorry that all these things happened to you. And I'm sorry I didn't notice sooner."

"Thanks, I guess," Jam replied.

“You know, a few years ago, I had a really unlucky day too,” explained Pam. “It wasn’t *this* bad, but still, it was pretty bad."

"I remember it was raining that day, and my umbrella blew away."

"And I forgot to close my backpack so all my stuff got soaked. Except for my lunch that is, because I forgot it at home."

"By the time school was done, I was hungry, wet and sad, and thought things couldn’t get any worse. And just then, I tripped on a rock and landed in a big puddle of mud.”

“Whoa, that *does* sound like a pretty bad day. So what did you do to make your bad luck go away?” asked Jam.

“Nothing,” Pam replied. “I mean, things didn't continue like that forever. Eventually, some good things happened again. But that’s just how it goes."

"Every day has good and bad parts. That day just had more bad parts."

"It’s kind of like the storm cloud that was raining on me. By the next day, it had passed and it was sunny again.”

"So you're saying, this won't last forever?" asked Jam.

"No, I don't think it will," replied Pam.

Then, for the first time since early that morning, Jam smiled.

“Thanks for being here with me, Pam,” said Jam. “I’m sorry I got so mad about the tacos. I know it’s your turn to choose dinner, so if that’s what you want, it’s fine with me.”

Pam was glad her brother was feeling a little better, but after hearing all about his terrible day, she wanted to do something to help *his* storm cloud go away.

"That's alright Jam. It’s been a rough day. I think I’d rather have pizza instead!"

Made in the USA
Monee, IL
18 February 2022